Fun Food for Cool Cooks

Banana-Berry Smoothies

AND OTHER BREAKFAST RECIPES

by Brekka Hervey Larrew

Capstone press®

Mankato, Minnesota

Snap Books are published by Capstone Press,
151 Good Counsel Drive, P.O. Box 669, Mankato, Minnesota 56002.
www.capstonepress.com

Library of Congress Cataloging-in-Publication Data
Larrew, Brekka Hervey.
    Banana-berry smoothies and other breakfast recipes / by Brekka Hervey Larrew.
    p. cm. — (Snap books. Fun food for cool cooks)
    Summary: "Provides fun and unique recipes for breakfast including banana-berry smoothies,
crispy apple strudel, and stuffed French toast. Includes easy instructions and a helpful tools glossary
with photos" — Provided by publisher.
    Includes bibliographical references and index.
    ISBN-13: 978-1-4296-2015-4 (hardcover)
    ISBN-10: 1-4296-2015-3 (hardcover)
    1. Breakfasts — Juvenile literature. I. Title. II. Series.
TX733.L37 2009
641.5'2 — dc22   2008001760

Editor: Kathryn Clay
Set Designer: Juliette Peters
Photo Stylist: Sarah L. Schuette

Photo Credits:
All principle photography in this book by Capstone Press/Karon Dubke
Capstone Press/TJ Thoraldson Digital Photography, cooking utensils (all)
David Larrew, 32

1 2 3 4 5 6 13 12 11 10 09 08

PAGE 8

PAGE 14

PAGE 18

PAGE 22

PAGE 24

PAGE 26

TABLE OF CONTENTS

INTRODUCTION

SEEING STARS

When choosing a recipe, let the stars be your guide. Just follow this chart to find recipes that fit your cooking comfort level.

EASY: ★ ☆ ☆
MEDIUM: ★ ★ ☆
ADVANCED: ★ ★ ★

You just woke up, and your stomach is growling. It has been hours since you've eaten. While it might be easy to pour a bowl of cereal, you're looking for something tastier. This book has plenty of fun and delicious recipes. Soon you'll be scrambling eggs, frying bacon, or slicing fruit. Before long your stomach will be full, and you'll have enough energy to last all morning.

METRIC CONVERSION GUIDE

United States	Metric
¼ teaspoon	1.2 mL
½ teaspoon	2.5 mL
1 teaspoon	5 mL
1 tablespoon	15 mL
¼ cup	60 mL
⅓ cup	80 mL
½ cup	120 mL
⅔ cup	160 mL
¾ cup	175 mL
1 cup	240 mL
1 quart	1 liter

1 ounce	30 grams
2 ounces	55 grams
4 ounces	110 grams
½ pound	225 grams
1 pound	455 grams

Fahrenheit	Celsius
325°	160°
350°	180°
375°	190°
400°	200°
425°	220°
450°	230°

All good cooks know that a successful recipe takes a little preparation. Use this handy checklist to save time when working in the kitchen.

BEFORE YOU BEGIN

READ YOUR RECIPE

Once you've chosen a recipe, carefully read over it. Everything will go smoothly if you understand the steps and skills.

CHECK THE PANTRY

Make sure you have all the ingredients on hand. After all, it's hard to bake cookies without sugar.

DRESS FOR SUCCESS

Wear an apron to keep your clothes clean. Roll up long sleeves. Tie long hair back so it doesn't get in your way — or in the food.

GET OUT YOUR TOOLS

Sort through the cupboards and gather all the tools you'll need to prepare the recipe. Can't tell a spatula from a mixing spoon? No problem. Refer to the handy tools glossary in this book.

PREPARE YOUR INGREDIENTS

A little prep time at the start will pay off in the end.
- Rinse any fresh ingredients such as fruit and vegetables.
- Use a peeler to remove the peel from foods like apples and carrots.
- Cut up fresh ingredients as called for in the recipe. Keep an adult nearby when using a knife to cut or chop food.
- Measure all the ingredients and place them in separate bowls or containers so they're ready to use. Remember to use the correct measuring cups for dry and wet ingredients.

PREHEAT THE OVEN

If you're baking treats, it's important to preheat the oven. Cakes, cookies, and breads bake better in an oven that's heated to the correct temperature.

The kitchen may be unfamiliar turf for many young chefs. Here's a list of trusty tips to help you keep safe in the kitchen.

KITCHEN SAFETY

ADULT HELPERS

Ask an adult to help. Whether you're chopping, mixing, or baking, you'll want an adult nearby to lend a hand or answer questions.

FIRST AID

Keep a first aid kit handy in the kitchen, just in case you have an accident. A basic first aid kit contains bandages, a cream or spray to treat burns, alcohol wipes, gauze, and a small scissors.

WASH UP

Before starting any recipe, be sure to wash your hands. Wash your hands again after working with messy ingredients like jelly or syrup.

HANDLE HABITS

Turn handles of cooking pots toward the center of the stove. You don't want anyone to bump into a handle that's sticking off the stove.

USING KNIVES

It's always best to get an adult's help when using knives. Choose a knife that's the right size for your hands and the food. Hold the handle firmly when cutting, and keep your fingers away from the blade.

COVER UP

Always wear oven mitts or use pot holders to take hot trays and pans out of the oven.

KEEP IT CLEAN

Spills and drips are bound to happen in the kitchen. Wipe up messes with a paper towel or clean kitchen towel to keep your workspace tidy.

In a hurry? Smoothies are easy to make and take with you. They're perfect for busy school mornings or hot summer days.

BANANA-BERRY SMOOTHIES

WHAT YOU NEED

●● *Ingredients*

1 medium banana
½ cup strawberries, fresh or frozen
½ cup blueberries, fresh or frozen
2 cups vanilla yogurt
1 cup milk
1 tablespoon sugar

●● *Tools*

blender

dry-ingredient measuring cups

liquid measuring cup

measuring spoons

2 drinking glasses

1 Peel banana and put in a blender.

2 Add strawberries and blueberries to the blender.

3 Measure yogurt with a dry-ingredient measuring cup. Add yogurt to the blender.

4 Measure milk with a liquid measuring cup. Add milk to the blender.

5 Measure sugar with a measuring spoon. Add sugar to the blender.

6 Using the blender's puree setting, combine ingredients until smooth.

7 Pour the mixture into drinking glasses and serve.

8

No Blender? No Problem

You can make a great smoothie even if you don't have a blender. Just cut up the fruit on a cutting board. Fresh berries work best if you're not using a blender. Put fruit in a zip-top plastic bag. Add the remaining ingredients and close the bag. Squish the plastic bag with your hands until ingredients are combined.

Omelets are delicious, but they can be hard to cook and even harder to flip. Now you can make a delicious omelet in the microwave. Instead of flipping it, you just fold it over.

DIFFICULTY LEVEL: ★ ★ ☆
SERVING SIZE: 1

CHEESE AND SAUSAGE OMELET

WHAT YOU NEED

● ● *Ingredients*

2 (2–3 ounce) slices precooked sausage
2 eggs
2 tablespoons milk
½ teaspoon salt
¼ teaspoon pepper
½ tablespoon butter
¼ cup shredded cheddar cheese

● ● *Tools*

cutting board

paring knife

small bowl

whisk

glass pie pan

oven mitt

pot holder

spatula

paper towel

1 On a cutting board, cut sausage slices into small pieces with a paring knife.

2 Crack eggs into a small bowl and throw away shells. Add milk, salt, and pepper to the bowl. Beat ingredients together with a wire whisk.

3 Place butter in a glass pie pan. Microwave butter for 30 seconds or until melted.

4 Pour eggs into the pie pan. Cover pan with a paper towel. Microwave on high for 90 seconds.

5 Use oven mitts or pot holders to remove the pie pan from the microwave.

6 Sprinkle cheese and sausage pieces on half of the eggs. Fold the other half of the eggs over the cheese and sausage.

7 Microwave the omelet for 90 seconds. Use oven mitts or pot holders to remove pan from microwave. Use a spatula to move the omelet onto a plate.

Get Cracking

The world's largest omelet was made in 2002. The Lung Association in Ontario, Canada, cooked an omelet weighing more than 6,500 pounds (2.95 metric tons). More than 160,000 eggs were used. That's a lot of eggs to crack!

If you don't have a lot of time in the morning, you can still enjoy a tasty breakfast. Just make this recipe a day or two ahead of time. Store the bread in the fridge until you're ready to eat.

DIFFICULTY LEVEL: ★ ★ ☆
MAKES: 1 LOAF
PREHEAT OVEN: 350° FAHRENHEIT

SUGAR AND SPICE BANANA BREAD

WHAT YOU NEED

●● Ingredients

½ cup (1 stick) butter, softened
¾ cup sugar
3 overripe bananas
2 eggs
1 teaspoon vanilla extract
½ cup milk
2 cups flour
1 teaspoon baking soda
½ teaspoon salt
1 teaspoon cinnamon
1 teaspoon sugar

●● Tools

mixing bowl

rubber scraper

3 small bowls

fork

loaf pan

oven mitt

pot holder

nonstick cooking spray

1 In a mixing bowl, cream butter and sugar with a rubber scraper.

2 Peel bananas and place in a small bowl. Mash bananas with a fork and add to the mixing bowl.

3 Crack eggs into the small bowl and throw away shells. Add eggs, vanilla, and milk to the mixing bowl. Mix ingredients together with the rubber scraper.

4 In a second small bowl, stir together flour, baking soda, and salt. Add this mixture to the mixing bowl and stir ingredients together.

5 Spray loaf pan with nonstick cooking spray. Pour batter into the loaf pan.

6 In a third small bowl, mix together cinnamon and sugar. Sprinkle mixture over batter.

7 Bake for 50–60 minutes (see Trusty Tip). Use oven mitts or pot holders to remove pan from oven. Allow bread to cool for 20 minutes before eating.

Trusty Tip

Insert a toothpick into the loaf to see if the banana bread is done. If the toothpick comes out clean, the bread is done. If there's batter on the toothpick, let the bread bake 3 minutes and check again.

Go Bananas

This recipe calls for overripe bananas. That means the banana peels have started to become spotty and the fruit is soft. Overripe bananas work best for banana bread. They are easier to mash than bananas that are still green.

Summer is a great time to eat fresh berries. Celebrate the season with a healthy, colorful breakfast. These parfaits are naturally sweet, so you could even serve them as dessert.

DIFFICULTY LEVEL: ★ ☆ ☆
SERVING SIZE: 4

RED, WHITE, AND BLUE PARFAITS

WHAT YOU NEED

●● *Ingredients*

1 cup fresh strawberries
2 cups vanilla yogurt
2 cups cornflakes or granola
1 cup fresh blueberries
sunflower seeds (optional)

●● *Tools*

cutting board   paring knife

mixing bowl   mixing spoon

4 small serving dishes

1 Place strawberries on a cutting board. Use a paring knife to cut off stems. Slice strawberries into pieces.

2 In a mixing bowl, stir together yogurt and cereal with a mixing spoon. Spoon ¼ cup of the mixture into each serving dish.

3 Add ¼ cup blueberries to each serving dish.

4 On top of blueberries, add ¼ cup yogurt mixture to each serving dish.

5 Add ¼ cup strawberries to each serving dish.

6 Top off each serving dish with ¼ cup yogurt mixture. Sprinkle sunflower seeds on top. Serve immediately.

Berry Picking

Unripe berries can be disappointing to eat. Instead of tasting sweet and juicy, they can be hard or sour. Look for berries that are firm and brightly colored. If some blueberries are starting to look like raisins, find another package to buy. Check the package to make sure there's no mold. Remember to rinse all fruit before eating.

On a cool morning, nothing beats a warm biscuit.
Add ham and egg, and you've got a complete meal.

SUNNY BISCUIT BITES

WHAT YOU NEED

●● Ingredients

1 egg
1 microwaveable frozen biscuit
1 slice precooked ham

●● Tools

skillet

serrated knife

spatula

2 microwave-safe plates

nonstick cooking spray

1 Spray a skillet with nonstick cooking spray.

2 Crack egg into the skillet. Cook egg on medium heat until the egg white is firm and the yolk begins to thicken. Remove skillet from heat.

3 Place biscuit on a microwave-safe plate. Microwave biscuit according to package directions.

4 Remove plate from microwave. Cut biscuit in half with a serrated knife.

5 Place ham on a second microwave-safe plate. Microwave ham for 30 seconds or until warm.

6 Put ham on the bottom half of biscuit. Use a spatula to place egg on top of ham. Cover egg with top of biscuit.

For a cheesy twist, add a slice of cheddar or American cheese on top of the egg. You could also try precooked bacon or sausage in place of the ham. If you don't like eggs sunny-side up, try scrambled eggs instead.

Hotcakes, flapjacks, short stacks. Whatever you call them, pancakes are delicious. Add ginger ale and blueberries for an extra fluffy, fruity taste.

DIFFICULTY LEVEL: ★ ★ ★
SERVING SIZE: 7-9 PANCAKES

BERRY FIZZY PANCAKES

WHAT YOU NEED

•• *Ingredients*
1 egg
2 tablespoons olive oil
1 teaspoon lemon juice
½ cup buttermilk
1 cup flour
1 tablespoon sugar
1 tablespoon baking powder
½ teaspoon salt
2–3 tablespoons butter
½ cup fresh blueberries
⅓ cup ginger ale

•• *Tools*

mixing bowl   whisk

griddle   spatula

plate

1 Crack egg into a mixing bowl and throw away shell. With a whisk, beat egg until frothy.

2 Add olive oil, lemon juice, and buttermilk to the mixing bowl. Mix ingredients together with the whisk.

3 Add flour, sugar, baking powder, and salt to the mixing bowl. Mix ingredients together.

4 Place 1 tablespoon butter onto a griddle. Heat on medium until butter melts. Make sure the melted butter covers the entire surface of the griddle.

5 As the griddle is heating, stir the blueberries and ginger ale into the batter. Pour ¼ cup circles of batter onto the hot griddle.

6 Let the pancakes cook about 3 minutes. When bubbles form and pop on the pancakes, flip the pancakes over with a spatula. Cook for 3 minutes and remove pancakes with the spatula. Place pancakes on a plate.

7 Repeat steps 4–6 until all the batter is gone. Serve hot with butter, syrup, or whipped cream.

Pancake Day

In England, Pancake Day is celebrated on Shrove Tuesday. In the United States, this day is called Fat Tuesday. On Pancake Day, people in England celebrate with pancake races. Only women are allowed to participate. Each contestant wears a head scarf and apron. Racers must run the race while flipping pancakes on a griddle. The first pancake race was in Olney, England, in 1445.

If you love French toast, this is the perfect recipe for you. Add cream cheese and a fruity filling, and plain French toast becomes a fancy treat. It's the perfect breakfast to serve someone in bed.

DIFFICULTY LEVEL: ★ ★ ★
SERVING SIZE: 6

STUFFED FRENCH TOAST

WHAT YOU NEED

• • Ingredients

¾ cup maple syrup
¼ cup apricot preserves
1 loaf Italian bread
1 (8.75-ounce) can apricots
½ package (4 ounces) cream cheese, softened
1 tablespoon apricot preserves
6 eggs
6 tablespoons milk
½ teaspoon vanilla extract
½ teaspoon nutmeg
1–2 tablespoons powdered sugar

• • Tools

2 small bowls   mixing spoon   cutting board

serrated knife   paring knife   mixing bowl

whisk   skillet   spatula

nonstick cooking spray
plate

1 In a small bowl, combine maple syrup and apricot preserves with a mixing spoon. Set aside.

2 On a cutting board, cut the bread into six slices with a serrated knife. On the top of each slice, cut a slit halfway down to form a large pocket.

3 On the cutting board, chop the apricots into small pieces with a paring knife. In a mixing bowl, combine apricots, cream cheese, and 1 tablespoon preserves. Stir ingredients together with the mixing spoon. Scoop mixture into each bread pocket.

4 Crack eggs into a second small bowl and throw away shells. Add milk, vanilla, and nutmeg to the small bowl. With a whisk, beat the mixture until frothy.

5 Spray a large skillet with nonstick cooking spray. Dip bread into the egg mixture, wetting both sides. Place bread in the skillet and cook on medium heat until golden brown, about 4 minutes. Use a spatula to flip the bread over. Cook an additional 3 minutes.

6 Place the toast on a plate. Pour the syrup mixture over the toast. Sprinkle with powdered sugar.

Is French Toast Really French?

French toast was likely invented as a way to soften stale bread. But the French weren't the first to make this dish. Recipes for French toast can be traced back to ancient Rome. In France, one of the early names for this type of bread was *pain a la Romaine* (Roman bread). Now, the French commonly call it *pain perdu*, which means "lost bread."

Enjoy a traditional breakfast treat with a cheesy twist. These rollups taste so good, you'll want to share them with family and friends.

DIFFICULTY LEVEL: ★ ★ ★
SERVING SIZE: 8
PREHEAT OVEN: 375° FAHRENHEIT

BACON-CHEDDAR ROLLUPS

WHAT YOU NEED

●● *Ingredients*

4 slices bacon
1 (8-ounce) package crescent roll dough
1 cup finely shredded cheddar cheese

●● *Tools*

skillet   metal tongs

baking sheet   oven mitt

pot holder

plate
paper towel

1 Arrange bacon slices in a skillet. Cook bacon over medium-high heat. Turn the bacon over occasionally with metal tongs until bacon is browned and crispy. Put fully cooked bacon on a plate lined with a paper towel.

2 On a baking sheet, spread out the eight triangles of crescent roll dough. Crumble a half slice of bacon onto each triangle.

3 Sprinkle cheese over bacon.

4 Roll up dough according to the package directions. Bake for 11–13 minutes. Use oven mitts or pot holders to remove baking sheet from the oven.

5 Sprinkle tops of rollups with cheese.

Tasty Tip

Instead of using bacon strips, use 2 ounces of diced ham. Replace the cheddar cheese with Swiss cheese.

Quick Fix

Don't have a lot of time in the morning? Use precooked bacon instead. You'll get the same great taste without the wait.

If you like apple pie, then you will love this breakfast pastry. The strudel is filled with cinnamon apples and topped with butter. It's a flaky treat that will leave you licking your fingers.

DIFFICULTY LEVEL: ★ ★ ☆
SERVING SIZE: 6
PREHEAT OVEN: 400° FAHRENHEIT

CRISPY APPLE STRUDEL

WHAT YOU NEED

•• Ingredients

2 sheets of puff pastry
2 Granny Smith apples
¼ cup chopped walnuts
¼ cup raisins
¼ cup sugar
½ teaspoon cinnamon
½ teaspoon nutmeg
¼ cup (½ stick) butter
1–2 tablespoons powdered sugar

•• Tools

cutting board   vegetable peeler   paring knife

mixing bowl   mixing spoon   small bowl

microwave-safe bowl   baking sheet   oven mitt

pot holder

1 Remove two sheets of puff pastry from the freezer. Thaw pastry for 45 minutes.

2 On a cutting board, use a vegetable peeler to peel apples. With a paring knife, cut out cores and throw away. Cut remaining apple into small chunks. Place apple chunks into a mixing bowl.

3 Add walnuts and raisins to the mixing bowl. Stir ingredients together with a mixing spoon.

4 In a small bowl, mix sugar, cinnamon, and nutmeg. Pour this mixture over the apples and stir.

5 In a microwave-safe bowl, microwave butter for 30 seconds or until melted. Pour butter over apples.

6 Slice each sheet of pastry into three pieces. Place ½ cup apple filling on each piece. Fold pastry over the filling. Dip your fingers in water. Wet edge of the dough and seal pastry shut. Arrange on a baking sheet, about 1 inch apart. Bake for 15 minutes.

7 Use oven mitts or pot holders to remove pan from the oven. Sprinkle strudels with powdered sugar.

Did You Know?

Strudel is a German word that means "whirlpool." In Austria, strudels are a popular breakfast food. Common flavors include apple, cheese, and cherry.

Tasty Tip

For a creamier filling, add 4 ounces of softened cream cheese to the apple mixture.

You couldn't get away with eating a chocolate chip cookie for breakfast. But your mom probably wouldn't object to you eating a muffin. Eat them fresh out of the oven with a tall glass of milk.

DIFFICULTY LEVEL: ★ ★ ☆
MAKES: 12 MUFFINS
PREHEAT OVEN: 350° FAHRENHEIT

CHOCOLATE CHIP MUFFINS

WHAT YOU NEED

•• Ingredients
2 cups flour
½ cup sugar
1 tablespoon baking powder
½ teaspoon salt
1 egg
½ cup milk
⅓ cup oil
⅓ cup sour cream
1 cup mini chocolate chips
3 tablespoons sugar
3 tablespoons brown sugar

•• Tools

mixing bowl

mixing spoon

2 small bowls

paper baking cups

muffin pan

oven mitt

pot holder

1 In a mixing bowl, combine flour, sugar, baking powder, and salt with a mixing spoon.

2 Crack egg into a small bowl and throw away shell. Add egg to the mixing bowl.

3 Add milk, oil, and sour cream to the mixing bowl and stir ingredients together.

4 Mix in mini chocolate chips.

5 Put paper baking cups into a muffin pan. Spoon batter into baking cups, filling each ⅔ full.

6 In a second small bowl, mix together 3 tablespoons sugar and 3 tablespoons brown sugar. Sprinkle over the batter.

7 Bake for 15–20 minutes. Use oven mitts or pot holders to remove pan from the oven.

Tasty Tip

Instead of chocolate chips, add a cup of frozen blueberries. Replace sugar and brown sugar topping with a crumb topping. Mix together ¼ cup sugar, 2½ tablespoons flour, 2 tablespoons softened butter, and ¾ teaspoon cinnamon. Sprinkle mixture over batter before baking.

TOOLS GLOSSARY

baking sheet — a flat metal tray used for baking foods

blender — a small electric appliance with a tall plastic or glass container and metal blades

cutting board — a wooden or plastic board used when slicing or chopping foods

dry-ingredient measuring cups — round, flat cups with handles

fork — an eating utensil often used to stir or mash

griddle — a large, flat pan used to cook food

liquid measuring cup — a measuring cup with a spout for pouring

loaf pan — a baking pan used to bake bread

measuring spoons — spoons with small, deep scoops used to measure both wet and dry ingredients

metal tongs — a tool with connecting arms used to pick up or flip things over

microwave-safe bowl — a nonmetal bowl used in microwave ovens

mixing bowl — a sturdy bowl used for mixing ingredients

mixing spoon — a large spoon with a wide, circular end used to mix ingredients

muffin pan — a pan with individual cups for baking muffins or cupcakes

oven mitt — a large mitten made from heavy fabric used to protect hands when removing hot pans from an oven

paper baking cups — disposable paper cups that are placed into a muffin pan to keep batter from sticking to the pan

paring knife — a small, sharp knife used for peeling or slicing

pie pan — a glass or metal pan used to bake pies

pot holder — a thick, heavy fabric cut into a square or circle that is used to remove hot pans from an oven

rubber scraper — a kitchen tool with a rubber paddle on one end

serrated knife — a saw-toothed knife used to cut bread

skillet — a flat pan used to cook non-liquid foods on a stovetop

small bowl — a bowl used for mixing a small amount of ingredients

spatula — a kitchen tool with a broad, flat, metal or plastic blade at the end, used for removing food from a pan

vegetable peeler — a small tool with two blades used to remove peels from vegetables and fruits

whisk — a metal tool used for beating ingredients together

GLOSSARY

cream (KREEM) — to mix ingredients until soft and smooth

extract (EK-strakt) — a strong solution of liquid made from plant juice; vanilla extract is made from vanilla beans.

frothy (FRAW-thee) — foamy

parfait (par-FAY) — a cold dessert made by layering different foods

puree (pyoo-RAY) — the process of mixing two or more ingredients into a smooth sauce or paste

serrated (SER-ay-tid) — saw-toothed

yolk (YOKE) — the yellow part of an egg

Ibbs, Katharine. *DK Children's Cookbook.* New York: DK, 2004.

Kalman, Bobbie. *Breakfast Blast.* Kid Power. New York: Crabtree, 2003.

Wagner, Lisa. *Cool Meals to Start Your Wheels: Easy Recipes for Kids to Cook.* Cool Cooking. Edina, Minn: Abdo, 2007.

FactHound offers a safe, fun way to find Internet sites related to this book. All of the sites on FactHound have been researched by our staff.

Here's how:

1. Visit *www.facthound.com*
2. Choose your grade level.
3. Type in this book ID **1429620153** for age-appropriate sites. You may also browse subjects by clicking on letters, or by clicking on pictures and words.
4. Click on the **Fetch It** button.

FactHound will fetch the best sites for you!

ABOUT THE AUTHOR

Brekka Hervey Larrew began cooking with her mother when she was a little girl, mainly because she loved to eat (and still does). As a teenager, she held elaborate seven-course dinner parties for friends and relatives. Larrew baked as many varieties of cookies as she could find in recipe books. She has experimented with multicultural cooking and has spent a lot of time perfecting the art of baking pies.

Larrew taught elementary and middle school for 12 years. Currently, she stays home with her two children, both of whom help out in the kitchen. She lives in Nashville.

INDEX